WEATHER
Rain

by Ann Herriges

BELLWETHER MEDIA • MINNEAPOLIS, MN

Note to Librarians, Teachers, and Parents:

Blastoff! Readers are carefully developed by literacy experts and combine standards-based content with developmentally appropriate text.

Level 1 provides the most support through repetition of high-frequency words, light text, predictable sentence patterns, and strong visual support.

Level 2 offers early readers a bit more challenge through varied simple sentences, increased text load, and less repetition of high-frequency words.

Level 3 advances early-fluent readers toward fluency through increased text and concept load, less reliance on visuals, longer sentences, and more literary language.

Whichever book is right for your reader, Blastoff! Readers are the perfect books to build confidence and encourage a love of reading that will last a lifetime!

This edition first published in 2007 by Bellwether Media.

No part of this publication may be reproduced in whole or in part without written permission of the publisher. For information regarding permission, write to Bellwether Media Inc., Attention: Permissions Department, Post Office Box 1C, Minnetonka, MN 55345-9998.

Library of Congress Cataloging-in-Publication Data
Herriges, Ann.
  Rain / by Ann Herriges.
    p. cm. — (Blastoff! readers) (Weather)
Summary: "Simple text and supportive images introduce beginning readers to the characteristics of rain. Intended for students in kindergarten through third grade."
  Includes bibliographical references and index.
  ISBN-10: 1-60014-027-0 (hardcover : alk. paper)
  ISBN-13: 978-1-60014-027-3 (hardcover : alk. paper)
  1. Rain—Juvenile literature. 2. Weather—Juvenile literature. I. Title. II. Series.

QC924.7.H47 2007
551.57'7—dc22   2006000618

Text copyright © 2007 by Bellwether Media.
Printed in the United States of America.

Table of Contents

What Is Rain? 4

The Water Cycle 10

Floods and Droughts 18

We Need Rain 20

Glossary 22

To Learn More 23

Index 24

Rain is water that falls from **clouds**.

Rain is made up of raindrops.
Raindrops are many sizes.

Some raindrops are small and light. They fall slowly. Light rain is called **drizzle**.

Some raindrops are big and heavy. Heavy rain falls fast. *Splat!* The raindrops land hard.

Rain brings water to the
earth. It falls into rivers,
lakes, and oceans.

It soaks into the ground.

The water on Earth will become rain again. It turns into tiny drops called **water vapor**. The vapor rises into the air.

Water vapor drops are too small to see. They are so light that they float in the air.

The air rises and cools. The water vapor drops grow bigger.

The drops stick to **dust** in the air and make clouds.

The water drops inside a cloud bump into each other. The drops clump together to make bigger drops. The cloud turns dark.

The water drops become heavier than the air. They fall to the ground as rain.

Rain is part of the water cycle.
Rain or snow falls to the ground.
Water on the ground becomes
vapor and rises.

Clouds form. Rain or snow falls to the ground again. The water cycle never ends.

Too much rain can cause a **flood**. Floods destroy buildings and crops.

Too little rain can cause a **drought**. Lakes and rivers dry up. The soil becomes hard and cracked.

People, plants, and animals
need water.

Rain brings water to all living things.

Glossary

cloud—tiny drops of water or crystals of ice that float together in the air

drizzle—a light, misty rain; the raindrops in drizzle are small.

drought—a long time of dry weather without rain

dust—tiny bits of matter floating in the air

flood—when water covers land that is usually dry; rivers and lakes cannot hold all the water when too much rain falls.

water vapor—tiny drops of water that are small enough to float in the air; water vapor cannot be seen.

To Learn More

AT THE LIBRARY

Branley, Franklyn M. *Down Comes the Rain*. New York: HarperCollins, 1997.

Hesse, Karen. *Come On Rain*. New York: Scholastic, 1999.

Schaefer, Lola M. *This Is the Rain*. New York: Greenwillow Books, 2001.

Stojic, Manya. *Rain*. New York: Crown, 2000.

ON THE WEB

Learning more about the weather is as easy as 1, 2, 3.

1. Go to www.factsurfer.com

2. Enter "weather" into search box.

3. Click the "Surf" button and you will see a list of related web sites.

With factsurfer.com, finding more information is just a click away.

Index

air, 10, 11, 12, 13, 15

animals, 20

clouds, 4, 13, 14

drizzle, 6

drought, 19

dust, 13

Earth, 8, 10

flood, 18

lakes, 8, 19

oceans, 8

people, 20

plants, 20

raindrop, 5, 6, 7

rivers, 8, 19

soil, 19

water cycle, 16, 17

water vapor, 10, 11, 12, 16

The photographs in this book are reproduced through the courtesy of: Peter Cade, front cover; Carsten Peter, pp. 4-5; Andrew Doran, p. 5; Chris Windsor/Getty Images, p. 6; Jim Cummins/Getty Images, p. 7; Mike Magnuson/Getty Images, p. 8; Markusson Photo/Getty Images, p. 9; Joe Gough, p. 10; Christopher Pattberg, p. 11; Shaun Lombard, p. 12; AVTG, p. 13; Pete Turner/Getty Images, pp.14-15; National Geographic Survey, pp. 16-17; Alan Heartfield, p. 18; Paulus Rusyanto, p. 19; Beverly Joubert/Getty Images, p. 20(top), Milan Radulovic, p. 20(bottom); Steve Winter/Getty Images, p. 21.